PURPOSE FILLED
PARENTING

Teandra Gordon

ISBN 978-1-64028-953-6 (Paperback)
ISBN 978-1-64028-954-3 (Digital)

Christian Faith Publishing, Inc.
296 Chestnut Street
Meadville, PA 16335
www.christianfaithpublishing.com

Photo credit to Jade Stenger Photography.

Printed in the United States of America

Purpose Filled Parenting is a practical and informative handbook for parents on how to raise their children with meaningful intent. It provides parents with practical wisdom and helps them draw from their own childhood experiences which enables them to make better parenting choices for their own children. I frequently go back and reread a chapter when I come across a difficult parenting situation and I find different ways I can help to solve the problem. I find Purpose Filled Parenting is a valuable read for parents with children of any age.

Christy Galtney, Mother of 3

Acknowledgement

Thank you to my husband, Brian Gordon, parents, Vasteen Bailey and Theresa Broussard Bailey, and children, Brian, Tiara, Tayla, and Brielle Gordon for your unconditional belief in my dreams. With gratitude to Richard Henriksen, PhD, Tamisha Jones, MD and Chad Lemaire, MD for your mentorship and feedback on this project. A huge thank you to my research participants. You opened your hearts and homes and shared your stories. I hope that your stories will inform and enhance the lives of families all over the world.

Dr. Teandra Gordon

Foreword

I'm a pediatrician. In fact, I'm the medical director for the pediatric department of a large community health center. I should know a lot about kids. I should understand them fully. And most of the time I feel pretty confident about that…except if you're talking about my own three children. About a year ago, I was frustrated, tired and altogether done when I called to consult with Dr. Teandra Gordon, whom I have the great pleasure to know just as Teandra. I called her about an issue I was having at the time with my 9-year-old son, Cole. Our whole family had been displaced from our home due to a renovation, and the five of us were living in a one bedroom apartment above our garage. Cole had begun having melt downs at school. We had talked to him about the importance of school, cajoled and threatened him, but all attempts were unsuccessful. My husband and I always knew that our oldest son had a sensitive nature and we knew that our home-life situation, albeit temporary, was affecting him. The insight was there, but we weren't sure how to support him. Frustrated, I spoke with Teandra. As we were colleagues at the time, I prefaced our conversation by telling her that I had an issue of a personal nature. I explained our situation. After chatting about it for just a few minutes, I had a shift not just about our situation, but about my son in general. We had always spoken to him about "managing his emotions," but never about feeling them and understanding the strength in them. The feelings were not his kryptonite, but in fact, they were his super power.

I left the conversation understanding that it was my role to help him learn how to pause to allow his feelings to strengthen him. Cole was able to complete the rest of the school year (and our home renovation) with a better understanding of himself and additional tools for his "life" toolkit. My parenting felt more purposeful, too.

I met Dr. Teandra Gordon, about four years ago when I was the sole primary care physician in a small clinic filled with psychiatrists and therapists. I took a trip to the break room one day and found her door open on the way back. I paused to introduce myself and noticed the pictures of her four children. I found her disarmingly friendly and thoughtful—perfect qualities for a therapist. I would not see her again until I had been promoted to be the medical director of 7 school-based health centers. The program needed a director of therapy. Teandra was our last interview, and as soon as I saw her again I remembered those disarming qualities that had given me pause at our first meeting. It was clear that she would be a valuable addition to our team. Since that time—aside from her other jobs as mother, professor and motivational speaker—she has been the driving force of a successful school-based therapy team now serving 17 schools.

Much of what Teandra shared with me that day is captured so beautifully in her new work which follows. Anyone wishing to be a more spiritually, physically and emotionally present parent will benefit. Just as Dr. Gordon helped me understand and shift to more purposeful parenting, it is with great pleasure that I introduce you to *Purpose Filled Parenting!*

Tamisha E. Jones, MD

Introduction

Purpose Filled Parenting stems from the idea that great kids don't just happen, but that there are things that parents can do on purpose to foster an environment where kids can shine. Parenting is a thoughtful process that involves effort, planning, and sacrifice. Each child is different, so there are no step-by-step instructions to raising purpose filled kids. This book is aimed with providing parents with the essential ingredients that kids need for success. Maya Angelou said that "when you know better, you do better." I believe that as parents learn the essential ingredients to success, parents will utilize these concepts to give their children the optimal opportunity to reach their potential.

Parenting is the most difficult job in existence. It is twenty-four hours a day, seven days a week, and it carries a life-long commitment. I often hear parents say, "Kids don't come with an instruction manual." This is true! *Purpose Filled Parenting* is not an instruction manual, but it is replete with practical ideas, wisdom, and experiences. Becoming acquainted with the experiences and wisdom of others can help parents ask better questions and make more informed decisions for their children.

A parent's dream for their child is often rooted in that parent's own experiences. The chapters in this book are designed to help parents examine their own upbringing and utilize their experiences to make more informed choices for their children. Each child has their own path, but parents are tasked with the responsibility to put their child in the best position to discover their purpose. I hope that all parents develop a dream for their children. This dream is not what your child's career will be but the type of human that you want your child to become. *Purpose Filled Parenting* is designed to assist parents in developing a dream for their child and a blueprint to achieve it.

I became a first grade teacher after graduating with my bachelor's degree in Psychology. I taught elementary school for three years while working on my master's degree in Family Therapy. Following completion of my master's degree, I accepted a position as a Clinical Intervention Specialist with a grant-funded program called Safe4Kids. We worked in partnership with Child Protective Services to provide individual therapy, family therapy, and parenting education groups to families in the CPS system due to maternal substance abuse. After two years, I began work on my PhD and furthered my clinical experience as a therapist and then Director of Therapy Services at a large community health center in Houston, Texas, where I specialize in Pediatric Behavioral Health. My academic research was focused on minimizing the achievement gap among ethnic minority students and understanding essential ingredients to success in parenting. The core concepts in this book are derived from this work. I conducted qualitative research in which I interviewed parents about the factors that influenced their development and what they believe equates to success in parenting their own children. I have joined my research with both clinical and practical experiences to offer information that every parent should know!

Purpose Filled Parenting is based on a combination of academic research, experiences that I have had as a marriage and family therapist, and my personal experiences as a mom and daughter. It is packed with practical wisdom and combines both information and heart. I hope to walk alongside you in your parenting journey. This is truly a work from the heart that will engage both your head and your soul as you explore the essential ingredients to success in parenting and learn to parent your child "with purpose."

Contents

CHAPTER 1

The Parenting Relationship

"Love me like I'm your own flesh,
though I am separate and unique.
Hold me, see me, laugh with me;
in your heart I'll forever be."
—Dr. Teandra Gordon

The parenting relationship is a human-to-human connection that begins at birth and endures throughout a lifetime. From the moment they are born, children are in need of the presence, consistency, and communication of a loving caregiver. The connection between a parent and a child is significant. The nature of the connection changes as the child develops, but there are key factors that should remain consistent. In my research with parents regarding effective parenting strategies, parents identified the importance of presence, consistency, and communication in the parenting relationship. Healthy, happy relationships with our children make life more enjoyable and give children the foundation that they need for healthy development.

Human development researchers have attributed the formulation of the human personality to the infant-caregiver connection. When caregivers provide nurturance, closeness, and responsiveness to the needs of their infants, these infants develop a secure attachment with their caregivers. This secure attachment is the foundation for development in spirit, mind, body, and relationships.

Many parents worry about "spoiling" their newborns. Providing hugs, kisses, closeness, and warmth provides children with the security that they need to develop optimally. There's no such thing as too much love! When infants have a secure foundation, they experience safety, which allows them to explore their world, take risks, and develop in a way that helps them to actualize their potential as human beings.

The security of the parenting relationship is based on a foundation of unconditional love. Unconditional love communicates that "my love for you is not based on your actions and does not change according to whether you are making good or bad choices. My love for you just is...My love for you is based on the essence of who you are." When children are misbehaving, they should know that, though you may feel angry or disappointed, your love for them does not change. Unconditional love is love that is not moved by conditions. It is like a tree planted firmly in the ground that the wind and rain cannot uproot. A realization of love despite conditions sets the stage for a parent-child connection that can weather the storms of infancy, childhood, adolescence, and beyond. The world can be a difficult place where children can get beaten and bruised. Other children can be mean and judgmental at school. It can be tough to lose an election for class office or miss cuts for the basketball team. Home should be a safe place where those bruises can be nursed back to health. A healthy parent-child connection is paramount in creating a safe, nurturing home environment.

Presence

What does it mean to be present in your child's life? A participant in one of my research studies described it below:

"What I do know is that you need to be engaged and present with your kids, and when you're with them, you have to really be with them and not be distracted by cell phones or television, or even your own thoughts."

My study participants' sense of the relationship with their parents was embedded in how present they perceived their parents to be in their lives. Participants who identified a close relationship with their parents described their parents as "with me most of the time" or "always present."

"My dad bought me the ice skates, but [Mom] would take [me] ice skating."

"I remember as a kid, my dad would pick me up [every day from preschool] and we would go get Church's chicken. Then we would come back home and watch Fraggle Rock."

"[Following my parents' divorce, weekends with my dad] was all just very downtime. We would go on long bike rides and long walks and go to the movies...I was closer to him because of that."

On the other hand, participants who perceived a distant relationship with their parents described them as "just being very busy."

"She was there...I think she was doing stuff. I remember spending time with her, just not anything specific."

Life is busy. As parents, we have a myriad of responsibilities. On the top of our priority list should be spending quality time with our kids. It doesn't require lots of money, just a willingness to take extra steps to be present. Presence communicates significance. There is the old adage, "Put your money where your mouth is." Well I propose, "Put your time where your heart is." If the success of our children is our priority, being present with them must be a priority as well. Just as we *must* go to work and make dinner, at the top of our priority list *must* be spending quality time with our children. This does not mean that we are obligated to sacrifice career for the sake of parenting, just understand that our presence in our child's life is essential to his or her well-being. There is no magic formula for time spent a week, but the key is to communicate to your children that they are special, significant, and worthy of your time and attention. How this is communicated is different for different families.

Mothers, Fathers, and Sons

In a study that I conducted on raising black males, I interviewed fathers about the factors that influenced their development. Some men were raised in single mother households, while others were raised in two-parent households, but described their mothers as carrying on the majority of the daily childrearing responsibilities (taking them to and from school, helping them with homework, etc.). When these men discussed the influences on the men that they became, they talked about what they learned from their fathers. The participants discussed the "lessons" that their fathers taught them and what they learned from watching their fathers work and care for their families. The participants remarked:

My dad just always taught me to think differently about certain things.

My father would always preach on how to conduct yourself.

My father always told me the right thing. Everything that he would tell me would come to pass. And he was always nice. He wouldn't yell at me or curse at me or anything.

My dad didn't really instill a lot into me verbally. But now when I look at it, it was always his actions that were speaking louder than his words.

If my dad lived with me it would have been more structured. There would have been more consistency, and I probably would have made better choices.

There was no prerequisite for participants to have had a relationship with their father. The prerequisite was that participants lived in the same household with their children.

Interestingly, each male participant discussed a relationship with their father. I inferred that there is a correlation between being a present parent and having had a present parent. Role modeling is a powerful teaching tool. This in no way diminishes the influence of the mother on children's development. Mothers are the heart and soul of their family, and their consistent love and support are the heartbeat of their children, but fathers are a significant factor in male development.

Mothers, Fathers, and Daughters

Mothers were a source of inspiration for their daughters.

"My mother worked two and three jobs…she busted her butt all the time. I have never been afraid of hard work because I saw her do that."

"[My mother] always gave us the best, and she went without, so I learned self-sacrifice. For me, I'm willing to sacrifice anything for my kid."

These participants' mothers served as an example of womanhood and the values that the participants later espoused in adulthood.

For daughters, the father is a significant force in establishing positive self-esteem. A research participant described how a lack of relationship with her father affected her. I had "self-esteem issues, confidence, not knowing how to relate to a male, questioning is something wrong with me?" Children are egocentric. When something is right or wrong in their world, they often think they are the cause. Just as the presence of a positive parental relationship signifies importance, the lack of a parental relationship signifies unimportance.

Lacking the Presence of One or Both Parents

Lacking the presence of one or both parents leaves a void that should be understood and addressed by those that care for children. Both mothers and fathers make unique and significant contributions to children's lives. At times, the lack of a parental presence is due to factors such as death, which is beyond human control. Far too many times, children lack a relationship with their parent due to human decisions.

A research participant described how individuals who were not socialized by both parents can make a different choice with their own children.

"Even if there was an absence of your father…knowing the value of his presence through his absence helps versus having the attitude of 'my daddy was never around' and stopping right there."

It is important for individuals who were reared without the presence of both parents to process what this meant for them and to make a conscious choice to do things differently with their own children. A research participant shared:

"I think we can all sit back and look at what happened in [our] childhood [and question], what can we do to make it better as we go from generation to generation?"

When biological parents are not present, it is even more significant that children have positive role models and caregivers in aunts, uncles, grandparents, teachers, coaches, clergy, mentors, and other significant adults that are willing to live beyond themselves and serve as a positive influence in the life of a child.

Consistency

Consistency is a "steadfast adherence to the same principles." What are the values that you hope to impart into your children and how consistent are you at displaying these values in your words, actions, and essence? A participant described consistency from his perspective:

"What works in parenting is consistency. I think the most important thing that you can be as a parent, above everything else, is consistent. Because even if you love them with all you have but you're not consistent with that, you have a problem. Kids come to you looking for the rules to life, and giving them those rules and being consistent, to me, is the most important thing, and that's where the greatest opportunities for success or failure can come from."

The old adage, "Do as I say and not as I do," is ineffective in parenting. Our life, our actions, and our truth are the biggest example for our children. We are their greatest role models. We are the example for how to live, love, and interact with others. If we want our children to be successful, we should be successful. Becoming a parent does not mean it is time to quit school or stop fulfilling your dream. Parenting, indeed, involves a commitment to provide our children with basic needs, but pursuing our dream and passion is the greatest gift that we can give to our children. It shows our kids how to pursue their own. The values that we want to impart into our children must be displayed in us. If we want our children to graduate from college, we should graduate from college. If we want our children to tell us the truth, then we should tell the truth! The greatest lessons in life are caught, and when we consistently and authentically represent the values that we want espoused in our children, these values will typically be transcended.

Communication

"When we were growing up, it was always kids were seen and not heard, but we want to step back from that and give them the opportunity [to] express themselves and be heard, whether we agree with it or not."

There is a scene from the Eddie Murphy film, *Imagine That*, that I like to show in presentations. In the film, Eddie Murphy and his daughter are playing together, just being silly, when she opens up about her fears regarding a song that she has to sing at school. Her dad (Eddie Murphy) stops, listens, and spends time helping his daughter with her problem. It is such a great example of a strong parent-child relationship and how presence contributes to communication.

Communication is the interchange of thoughts, opinions, and information. Mutual respect and congruence in words and actions sets the stage for effective parent-child communication.

Respect is present when children are seen as equals, not in maturity or experience but in their value, feelings, and motivations. Children are small human beings with thoughts, feelings, and opinions. Honoring their voice sets the stage for a positive parent-child relationship.

Listening to your child's thoughts and opinions communicates worth. A research participant shared, "Even if we're talking about something that is a non-negotiable, I still want to know what [my child] thinks about it." Children with greater self-worth are more successful and make better decisions regarding behavior and relationships. In my studies, the participants aimed to foster an environment that evoked open communication with their children.

"That's one thing that I want to be different. I want [my kids] to know they can come talk to me. I do have a softer side. I didn't see my dad's softer side until I was a teenager...I [want to] seem more human. I want them to know that I'm on you, but you can always come talk to me...Sometimes I feel like my parents, they talked at us, not to us. There were times when I just want [them] to talk to me, not talk at me. I don't even want you to

solve the problem; I just want you to listen. So I think listening to your kids and talking to them and letting them…express themselves."

"I have more of a communication and an open dialogue with my son because that's what I wanted, so I'm going to give him more understanding…One thing I said I'd do my best to never do is to tell my kids, 'Because I said so.' That's not a response I wanted, that's not a response I would want them to have."

"[My daughter's] thoughts and feelings matter, and I want this home to be an environment where she knows her thoughts and feelings matter and that she can share them. And even if we don't agree with them, we still value her enough that she has a place to do that."

"Be their best friend. Make sure they can talk to you about anything. Don't shelter them away from the reality of life. As they progress in their age, there is more that you can let them experience and tell them about. Don't try to hide things from them. Let them be able to come and talk to you about anything. You have to be aware of what they are saying. The main thing [is]…have a good relationship with them."

Sibling Relationships: "I Have More Than One Child!"

Having more than one child can complicate the one-on-one parenting relationship with each child, but sibling relationships add depth to children's lives. A parent that I interviewed was an only child. He expressed:

"So there are definitely times when you wish you had a sibling because it's somebody that you can talk to. You really grow up trial and error on your own. You don't really have someone to guide you and show you how things really worked. When [my mom] had me, there was a low chance for her to have [a baby], so for her to just have me was a blessing. But I want my daughter to have a sibling. I want her to experience having somebody else

to grow up with. I think that's a valuable thing to have. Not just from a family perspective, but also you learn how to communicate with other people, conflict resolution, conflict management…social things like that. I definitely want that for her."

Having more than one child does not mean that a special parenting relationship cannot exist with each child. I have four children, and my goal is to love each one like they're my favorite because they really are! Each child is special and unique and deserves a one-on-one connection with us. We shouldn't compare our children to each other. As parents, we can ensure that each child has an experience each day where we look them in the eye and connect.

Reminding our children that they are loved and seen each day only takes a moment.

It is also important to encourage children to have positive relationships with each other. My children are not allowed to physically fight each other or fight with their words. Negative name-calling is unacceptable. I consistently reinforce this value. A participant in my study reflected:

"I want [my children] to be able to feel like home life was a good thing and that being around the family was something that they enjoyed."

There will be inevitable conflict, but it is important to teach your children to avoid saying things that really hurt. Closeness will not occur if children are bullied by their siblings.

Another participant expressed that he wanted his family to be "just more of a family." He recalled that in his family of origin.

"You could see the divide there, you knew there was love, but you could see the divide in the house. So I don't want that for my family. I want us to be close-knit."

We should teach our children how to treat each other. We should set an expectation that our kids treat their siblings with kindness and respect. A couple in my research stressed the importance of fostering a good sibling relationship between their children. They teach their children:

"Love your brother. Love your sister. Take care of your sister... You're the big brother, you watch her. You protect her. Always love each other."

Parent with Purpose by Fostering a Strong Parent-Child Relationship

- *Have "special time" each day.* For young children, get down on the floor and give your child your undivided attention for a period of time each day. Go into their world, play with their favorite toys, and follow their lead. For older children and teenagers, be sure that each day includes time to connect with them. The key is to communicate love and maintain connection by listening to your children and letting them know that you enjoy their company.

   Working on the parent-child relationship through special time will ensure that your children do not have the same childhood memories as two of my study participants.

"She was there...I think she was doing stuff. I remember spending time with her, just not anything specific."

"My memory of [my mom] is just being very busy...it was always just doing stuff. Like we have to get this done and go here and I have to take them here and take them here... Now [that I'm an adult], it's completely opposite where I'm much closer to my mom. I talk to my mom almost every day."

It is important that our children have significant memories of laughing with us, playing with us, and learning from us. It takes purposeful action to communicate to our children that we are present in their lives.

- *Start nurturing routines for morning, dinner, and bedtime.* Get up a few minutes earlier to avoid yelling and chaos (as much as possible) and try to make mornings a pleasant time for the family. For dinner: turn off the TV, put away electronics, and talk to each other. At bedtime, pray together and/or read together. The goal is enjoying pleasant experiences, and the key word is *together.*"
- *Greet your children with a huge smile when they walk into a room.* As parents, we can have a critical eye and point out problems (e.g. Are you planning to wear those shoes with that outfit?) before acknowledging the value in our children's presence. Look at your child. Acknowledge their amazing presence. Smile at them and let them know that you are happy to see them.
- *Talk to your children about their day.* Sometimes just asking, "How was your day?" is too vague. Try sharing the rose and thorn of your day. You and your children each share the best thing that happened to you that day and the worst thing that happened to you that day. Share your humanity (on a level that your child can understand). Let them see you as a person and work to understand who they are as people.
- *Hang out and Play Together.* Have fun! Plan movie nights. Dance in the living room. Go to the park. Play freeze tag, basketball, or go on a run or walk. Spending active time outdoors can keep everyone healthy while simultaneously promoting close family relationships.

What is your plan for building a strong relationship with your child?

_____

_____

_____

_____

_____

CHAPTER 2

Self-Esteem

"I am perfectly flawed—a masterpiece;
with my strengths and weaknesses, I'm perfectly me."

Dr. Teandra Gordon

Am I enough? Do I matter? These are the questions asked when addressing self-esteem.

Is who I am enough to deserve love, success, life, and joy? Believing "I am enough" is the foundation to a healthy life. Our children's answer to the question, "Am I enough?" is first shaped by their parents and caregivers. As parents, we have the opportunity to speak life, joy, love, and success into our children's lives. Our words and actions communicate to our children whether they are smart, funny, talented, loveable, and fabulous or bad, stupid, annoying, and lazy. The words that we say to and about our children shape the view that they have about themselves. We should be thoughtful, purposeful, and positive when talking to and about our kids.

Each human being is marvelously designed. Our height, weight, hair texture, features, voice, personality and temperament are all perfectly fit for our distinct destiny and purpose. Children's self-esteem is largely shaped by their caregivers' understanding and expression of how special and significant they are. The words that we say about our kids are the words that they begin to believe about themselves! It is vitally important that we use positive words to describe our children.

Each human being is born with attributes that can be perceived as both positive and negative. As parents, we can choose to accentuate the positive or the negative, and what we give attention to will expand. A dad in one of my studies discussed his thoughts on his daughter's self-esteem.

"I want [my daughter] to be her own person and to be independent. I don't want her to be exposed to all kinds of crazy stuff before she is able to mentally handle it but to be able to think for herself and to be okay with being by herself. She should definitely know that she's loved. Being a girl, an African American girl, I want her to know that she is beautiful and that she's precious and unique and she's special and to not to let what society thinks to negatively influence her mindset."

One of the first activities I do with kids (and often adults) that I see in therapy is the "I Am" activity. In this activity, I have the client write their name or draw a picture of themselves in the middle of a paper and surround their name or picture with positive self-attributes. They identify these attributes on their own. If the client struggles to identify positive attributes, I read a list of attributes to them, and they pick out the ones that describe them. Some kids really grapple with this activity because they have heard negative labels attached to their identity. I push these clients to identify the positive. We then turn the positive self-attributes into "I Am" statements. I have the client read "I Am" before each positive self-attribute. I tell them to recite their statements each morning and night. I tell them that it is important for them to show their parents, teachers, family members, and other students who they really are. I encourage them to make choices that line up with who they are, and I frequently remind them until they start to believe it.

I once had a young man in therapy who viewed himself as dumb. He had been diagnosed with a learning disability and made F's in school. When I met him, I saw him as intelligent and gregarious, but he didn't view himself in a positive light. The "I Am" activity opened the door for him to hold a different perspective of his identity. When the door was opened for him to define his identity, he defined himself as smart. His grades immediately changed to A's and B's with no learning aids or special accommodations. This activity was the single intervention that changed his academic performance. It's not always this easy, but change only happens externally when we believe that it is possible internally. We have to believe that *we can* before we can accomplish any goal.

The summer before my freshmen year in high school, I made a list of the words that I wanted others to use to describe me as a high school student. It wasn't until I was out of high school that I realized if you talked to someone that knew me in high school, they would probably describe me with the very words that I wrote down the summer after my eighth grade year. Our thoughts, perceptions, and words are extremely powerful. Let's work to ensure that our children use the power of thought, perception, and words in a way that will empower them to reach their potential.

As a mother of four, I have had countless moments when I thought, *What is wrong with this child?* In the midst of tantrums and defiance, children can be challenging. It is vitally important to refrain from using negative terminology to describe our children's being. We are not always in control of the thoughts that enter our minds about our children, but we should stay in control of the words that come out of our mouths to describe them. Knowledge of child development is very important. Many of the negative behaviors that children demonstrate are normal for their developmental stage. Below is a brief guide to child development and a framework for understanding children's behavior at different stages. Your pediatrician is also a great source for information and insight into the developmental stages of children.

Infants: 0 to 1 Years Old

In the first year of life, babies need nurturance, closeness, stimulation, and attention. Children should form a secure attachment with their caregivers. When children feel loved and cared for, they learn to trust that their world is safe enough to explore and interact. It is important for parents to cuddle, play, and talk to their babies. When my children were babies, I talked to them like they could understand me. I walked through the grocery store talking to them about our grocery list. Others may have thought I was crazy, but these types of interactions contribute to language acquisition. Their little brains are always growing and developing, and interactions with those that care for them is significant to their development.

Below are tips for parenting your baby *with purpose*:

- Talk to your babies. Use words to describe the objects that they encounter.
- Sing to your babies. Though you may not be blessed with beautiful vocals, your babies will find your singing calming. To this day, my children believe that I have a beautiful voice and love to hear me sing (though they are the only ones)!
- When your baby makes sounds, repeat the sounds back to them and add words. This will help with language acquisition.
- Read to your baby. It is a time of bonding and can set the stage for them to enjoy this activity in the future.
- Say kind words to your baby in a kind tone of voice. Look your baby in the eye and let him or her experience the love in your face.
- Enjoy cuddling your baby because pretty soon they will be moving around, and cuddle time will be on their terms.
- Take your baby for regular checkups and build a positive relationship with your pediatrician. Ask questions and pay attention to the child safety and health information that pediatricians provide.

Toddlers: 1 to 2 Years Old

In the second year of life, your child will tend to become more mobile. They are eager to explore their world, may show defiant behavior, and begin to communicate more clearly.

Toddlers show greater independence and learn from the behavior of those around them. At this stage, it is critically important to watch the words that you say and the things that you do because your toddler will be watching, learning, and imitating.

Below are tips for parenting your toddler *with purpose*:

- Allow your child to grow in their new independence. Take a few extra moments and let them zip their own jackets, snap their own shoes, and feed themselves.
- Encourage your child to explore new things.
- Read, play, and communicate.
- Teach through redirection and praise (learn more about this in the "Guiding Behavior" chapter).
- Take your toddler for regular checkups. Build a positive relationship with your pediatrician.

Ask questions and pay attention to the child safety and health information that pediatricians provide.

Preschool: 3 to 5 Years Old

The preschool age is a wonderful stage of discovery and learning. Children need consistency in routines, expectations, and strategies utilized to guide their behavior. This is a significant time of learning and developing behavioral patterns that will set the stage for their future. Children continue to assert independence, and this can be fostered in a positive way by allowing your child to make controlled choices for themselves. (Would you like to wear this outfit or this outfit today? Would you like to have apples or oranges for a snack?) During the preschool years, "Why?" may become a favorite question. Preschoolers are seeking a deeper understanding of their world and experiences. Your preschooler may often challenge authority. It is important to stay consistent with expectations and follow through on promised consequences. Don't get into a battle of wills with your preschooler; just stay calm and consistent.

Below are tips for parenting your preschooler *with purpose*:

- Continue reading to your child and nurturing development in their own reading abilities.
- Allow your child to assist with chores and teach them at every opportunity.
- Speak to your child in complex sentences to assist with the expansion of their vocabulary (except when giving instructions; instructions should be clear and concise).
- Help your child learn to manage their emotions through modeling and coaching them through difficult experiences and emotions.
- Take your child for regular (often yearly) checkups and build a positive relationship with your pediatrician. Ask questions and pay attention to the child safety and health information that pediatricians provide.

Middle Childhood: 6 to 8 Years Old

In middle childhood, children develop deeper connections to the world and peer experiences. They develop intellectually, have more words to articulate their experiences, and show more empathy for others. Friendships become increasingly important, and children must navigate a social world. Parents should help children maintain confidence in their identity, likeability, and ability to succeed in physical, social, emotional, and intellectual capacities.

Below are tips for parenting *with purpose* during middle childhood:

- Provide consistent nurture, support, and encouragement. Help your child develop responsibility by giving him or her tasks such as setting the table, clearing the table, or keeping their rooms clean.
- Maintain consistent and open communication with your child. Talk to them about friends, school, and their future.
- Help develop your child's moral capacity by instilling values such as respect and compassion.
- Help your child set his or her own achievable goals and strategies for attaining them.
- Help your child solve problems and develop positive habits.
- Be clear and consistent with expectations and consequences. Set limits regarding routines, including TV, video games, and bedtime.
- Stay involved with your child's school. Meet teachers, staff, and understand learning goals and how you can partner with teachers to help your child achieve.
- Continue reading to your child. As your child learns to read, take turns reading to each other.
- Encourage your child to participate in extracurricular activities and provide the support for them to do so.

Older Childhood: 9 to 11 Years Old

Now your child is headed toward adolescent years! Friendships are very important to them at this stage in development. Children may begin to face peer pressure, and a healthy self-esteem and connection to family are protective factors that contribute to your child making positive choices. At this stage, children are more capable of understanding complex experiences and taking on the perspective of others. It is significant that children become more responsible while still experiencing the support and encouragement of their parents.

Praise, logical consequences, and losing privileges are significant strategies for guiding your child's behavior at this stage (see more in the "Guiding Behavior" chapter). Puberty is fast approaching, and children may begin to experience the physical changes associated with it (especially girls). Teach your children about proper self-care and hygiene to care for their changing bodies.

Below are tips for parenting your preteen *with purpose*:

- Spend time with your child. Talk with him or her about friends, accomplishments, and the challenges that they will face.
- Stay involved with your child's school. Go to events and develop trusting relationships with their teachers and school staff.
- Show your child unconditional love and affection and spend quality time together as a family.

Adolescence: 12 to 14 Years Old

Welcome to the wonderful world of adolescence! Your child is experiencing many changes physically, emotionally, intellectually, and socially. Your child is starting to develop their own identity and learning to believe what they believe because they believe it and not because of what others say. This is a time to respect their new independence, but stay close. Continue to communicate and hang out with your child. Get to know them and help them understand the world and their place in it. The dreaded peer pressure associated with sex, drugs, and alcohol may begin or intensify at this stage. Keep your adolescent involved in positive extracurricular activities so that their energy and passion are exerted in a positive direction. Pubescent changes in girls include menstruation, growing breasts, and pubic hair. Boys grow facial hair, pubic hair, and their voices become deeper. Accompanying these changes can be new insecurities about their looks and their bodies. Your adolescent may fluctuate between confidence and insecurity. Their hormones are changing, and they may become moodier and rude or short-tempered with family. Understanding that these are typical occurrences in this stage of development can help, though it is important that your adolescent is accountable for his or her actions.

Below are tips for parenting your adolescent *with purpose*:

- Meet and get to know your teen's friends and their families (as much as possible).
- Be honest and direct when talking with your teen about drugs, alcohol, and sex. Set expectations and give reasons for expectations. Always listen and be open to the ideas, experiences, and opinion of your teens.
- Stay interested and involved in your teen's school life.
- Listen to your teen and respect their ideas and opinions. It is significant that they feel heard.
- Be clear and consistent about goals and expectations (e.g. be respectful, make good grades, help with housework), but allow your teen to give input on how to reach those goals (when and how to study or clean).

Adolescence: 15 to 17 Years Old

Your teen is likely very willful and opinionated at this stage. They are deep into developing their own identity and may challenge long-held family ideals. Adolescence is a time when teens are coming into their own and learning to believe what they believe because they believe it and not just because you told them to believe it. Work to maintain a positive relationship with your teen by planning family vacations and activities that help maintain connection. Stay involved in school and extracurricular activities. Your teen will likely be leaving home soon and needs to learn all the skills necessary to make good choices and care for themselves when they are away from you. Teach them practical skills and share with them the wisdom that you have acquired throughout the years.

Below are tips for parenting your teen *on purpose*:

- Talk openly to your teen about sex. Share your values, but be open to listen to their ideas and experiences. If your teen is sexually active, be sure you seek medical consult and work to protect them against sexually transmitted diseases and unwanted pregnancies.
- Talk to your teen about the consequences of drugs and alcohol. Warn your teen against drinking and driving and urge them to never ride in the car with a friend that has consumed drugs or alcohol. Always give your teen a way out (e.g. communicate that they can call you at any time to pick them up if they find themselves in a questionable scenario).
- Know where your teen is and have a way to reach them. Ensure that he or she always has a way to reach you or another safe adult.
- Discuss Internet usage, text messaging, and social media.
- Know your teen's friends and talk to your teen about the significance of having friends with similar values.
- Encourage your teen, compliment them, and let them know that you believe in them.
- Create opportunities to communicate with your teen in a relaxed environment. Listen to them and value their opinions and ideas.
- Stay connected to your teen and be aware of what is going on in their life and relationships. Depression can be rampant at this stage of development. Suicide is the third leading cause of death among individuals aged fifteen to twenty-four. If you notice your teen become increasingly withdrawn, irritable, losing interest in activities that they have previously

enjoyed, crying frequently, expressing hopelessness, these may be signs of depression. Ask your teen about their emotional experiences and the extent of their emotional pain. Ask your teen directly if they have thoughts about suicide or self-harm. Asking won't give them ideas that they wouldn't have already known about, but it will give them the opportunity to open up to you. Seek professional help if your teen admits to suicidal thoughts, self-harm, or has enduring depressive symptoms.

Promoting Self-Esteem

A participant in one of my studies expressed that:

"Every child is different. When you speak about individual things, it is different with each child. So you have to understand your child, who they are, and then kind of gear your parenting style to them."

Every human being is special, and their development is unique, but there are commonalities within various developmental stages. Knowing what to expect of your child at different ages and stages can help you understand that many of their actions and experiences may be associated with their developmental stage. Knowing that teens can be rude and opinionated helps you understand that you are not alone, your child is not the devil's spawn, and there is hope in the next developmental stage!

Each human being has both positive and negative attributes. As parents, we can choose to accentuate the positive or the negative and what we give attention to will expand. This does not mean to ignore if teachers, administrators, or doctors are noticing that your child's experience or behavior at a certain developmental stage is not typical. Your child may have Down's syndrome, ADHD, Autism, or learning differences, but it does not change the fact that your child is special, significant, and has a purpose for their existence.

Learn about their diagnosis and always believe in the best possible scenario. Hope is a powerful motivator, and people defy the odds each day due to unrelenting optimism and unbreakable belief. Even in the midst of these diagnoses, our children are human beings with strength, beauty, and purpose.

The words that kids use to describe themselves should start a positive tape recorder in their mind—"I am smart," "I am gifted," "I am talented." These words are the precursors to "I can do this," which makes any task surmountable because they believe in themselves and in their ability to succeed. This ability is not just in some children but in all. Children have different strengths and weaknesses, but each child was born to make a positive and meaningful contribution to their environment and the people in their life. When parents start to believe in their children, then children start to believe in themselves.

The world can be a challenging place. Other kids can be mean, and authority figures can be harsh. It is important for home to be a safe haven. Home should be a place where children can know that after a rough day, they will be nurtured, comforted, encouraged, and uplifted. It is vital for children to feel loved and valued each day. This type of environment promotes a positive self-esteem, which leads to children who reach their potential.

You cannot give to others what you don't first have for yourself. Take the time to create a personal "I Am" list. What words do you want your kids, your spouse, your family, your coworkers, and others who know you to use when describing you? Write these words down and begin to say them each day with the words "I Am" before it. After a couple of weeks, make the same type of list with your kids. Have them identify positive self-attributes and turn them into "I Am" statements. Have your kids come up with their own words or pull from the list below and rewrite on another sheet of paper. Have your child read each word with the words "I Am" before it each day until it becomes part of who they are and the expectations that they hold for their choices.

Smart	Nice	Kind	Athletic	Artistic
Thoughtful	Organized	Insightful	Loving	Gifted
Musical	Creative	Hard-working	Energetic	Flexible
Strong	Courageous	Bold	Handsome	Beautiful
Talented	Intelligent	Special	Unique	Honest
Compassionate	Confident	Generous	Funny	Loyal
Trustworthy	Inspiring	Gentle	Adorable	Cute
Playful	Optimistic	Sweet	Pleasant	Responsible

CHAPTER 3

Discipline and Guiding Your Child's Behavior

"A world with social rules,
teach me to navigate.
I'll learn from your example
and inevitably stumble along the way."
Dr. Teandra Gordon

Healthy discipline involves a balance of both nurturance and guidance. Discipline is about teaching, training, preparing, and building skills within your child so that he or she is able to show self-control. It is about creating guidelines that not only encourage good choices but also teaching why it is important to make good choices. A research participant in one of my studies described their goal as wanting to "reinforce the importance of managed behavior" and for their children to be "able to conduct themselves in public and know how to speak to people." Whatever your particular goals, effective discipline is built on the presence of love and like between you and your child. The more a child likes you, the more they will want to please you by doing what you expect. Effective discipline grows from a human-to-human connection and a strong relationship between parent and child.

Kids thrive in environments in which they experience unconditional love but also clear expectations and stability. Kids may not always appreciate structure at the time but will appreciate it as they mature. A participant in my research study remembered:

"So growing up, my friends, none of them had their daddy around, so they could do whatever they wanted to do. And I was, like, "I got this dude at home telling me what I can and can't do." So I went through that period where you don't appreciate it, not realizing that he's training me to do what's right."

Respect is a word that continues to arise when parents discuss guiding their children's behavior.

"If there is one thing that I can do for them as a parent, it is [teach them] respect—have respect not just for the people around you but also for yourself."

Parents often come into my therapy office angry due to the lack of respect that their children show them. The truth is that respect stems from relationship. The stronger the parenting relationship, the more likely it is that children will show respect. Children want to please people that they like. In therapy, parents are amazed at how quickly their children respond to the limits that I set in session. This occurs because one of my first objectives in therapy is to build a relationship with both the parent and child. The child and I build a relationship that involves mutual respect as human beings, and from that relationship, children want to hear what I have to say.

Effective discipline is not about punishment. It is about creating an opportunity for your child to analyze the choice that they made and helping to guide them to make a better choice next time. Guiding our children's behavior is about teaching them the difference between good choices and bad choices and creating opportunities for our children to learn from their behavior and make better choices next time. Discipline is not about power and control; it is about teaching and training.

When discipline is about power and control, everyone loses. Children who behave a certain way in front of their parents due to fear behave differently when their parents are not around. The goal is not for children to consistently exhibit outward respect but for respect to emanate from a genuine place from within. Respect from a child is given to parents who respect themselves and respect their children. Many adults cringe at the idea of showing respect to children, but respect is given when respect is received. If we are our child's greatest role model, then a parent who models respect for themselves and others, including their children, will be more likely to have children who show respect for their parents and others.

Showing respect to your child means that you value their worth as human beings and you want to understand the motivations behind their actions, listen to their thoughts, ideas, and opinions, and view them as equal to you. A participant in my work echoed this sentiment:

"I want to be sure that I give them guidance but not in a controlling way where they don't think that I respect their opinion and their thoughts."

Parents maintain the authority to make decisions, but it is significant to honor your child's experience, ideas, and opinions as you make those decisions for your family. Respect means that there is not a double standard of behaviors and expectations. It means that you recognize that how you treat your child is how you are teaching them to treat you and others. A research participant described why respect is so important for him to instill in his children.

"Because that's where it starts; if you can respect yourself, then you will be able to respect others. And there's so many things that go along with it. Because when people see [respect] within your spirit, there are so many things that happen. People open doors for you, and you don't even have to say a word."

Self-Esteem and Discipline

As parents, we must separate the negative behaviors from the child. Your child is not "bad"; she made a bad choice. He is not a "liar"; he lied. If my essence is that "I am bad," I cannot escape that. If I made a "bad choice," I have the opportunity to make a different choice next time. If I am a "liar," then all I can do is lie. If I am an honest person that told a lie (or string of lies), then next time I can choose to tell the truth. Separating the negative behavior from the child gives the child the opportunity for change.

We want our children to experience guilt over their bad choices, not shame. Guilt leads to admission, an apology, and a desire to make better choices next time. Shame believes the negative "I Am" and gives no room for hope or change. Shame leads to negative perceptions, negative behavior, negative words, and negative outcomes. Shame is not the answer to improved behavior. Improved behavior occurs through recognizing that our "I Am" is better than the choices that we are making. Through this revelation, we make better choices.

Emotional Control

A key to effectively guiding our children's behavior is for parents to maintain emotional control. If everyone is angry and out of control, then nothing positive is being accomplished.

Self-care is the key to emotional control for parents. Unfortunately, this is an area where I need to practice what I preach! I have four children, a demanding job, and regularly give more than I am replenishing myself. When this occurs, I become weary, cranky, and emotional. Self-care is significant because you can't give to others what you don't first have for yourself. A few strategies for maintaining emotional control are:

- Develop a morning routine that prepares you for the day—reading a devotional, favorite quote, prayer, meditation.

- Get enough rest, eat healthy foods, exercise.
- Walk away from the situation.
- Take three to five slow, deep breaths.
- Positive self-talk.

Caring for yourself means caring for your children. When you can bring your best self into the relationship, it fosters a positive parent-child connection.

Upward Mobility

Parents often discipline their children the way they were disciplined. The parents in my studies described improving upon how they were raised in their interactions with their children.

"With every generation, we improve or try to enhance on whatever we were given before."

"Realizing I don't want to do the same exact thing. I have to figure out a way to be better. We can all sit back and look at what happened in [our] childhood [and question], what can we do to make it better as we go from generation to generation?"

Think about the strategies that your parents used to discipline you and analyze their effectiveness. Did you behave a certain way in front of your parents and differently when they were not around? Did you wish that your parents had provided you with more structure and guidance? Did you wish that your parents had listened more? Think about how your parents' techniques for guiding your behavior affected you and consider improving upon them. As a research participant eloquently articulated:

"With every generation, we improve or try to enhance on whatever we're given before."

Below are strategies to add to your discipline toolbox. These are tried and tested methods that, when coupled with a strong parent-child relationship, are effective tools in guiding children's behavior. Pick out one or two and begin to implement today!

Strategies for Guiding Your Child's Behavior

Praise. When you catch your child doing something right, praise them for it (ex. I love the way you shared that toy with your brother!). When you focus on what you want your child to do, then you will begin to see more of that behavior! Children will do anything for their parents' attention. If children only get that attention when they are in trouble, they will get in trouble to get attention. If they get attention when they make good choices, they will make more good choices to get more attention! I call "praise" my "teacher trick." I spent three years as an elementary school teacher. When I wanted to get my students' attention, I would pick out a student that was listening and say, "Ooooh, I love the way Johnny is looking at me. He has his hands on his desk, his feet on the floor, his mouth closed, and his ears open. Thank you so much, Johnny, for listening to me." I then pick out another student who is meeting expectations and call them out. Before you know it, the entire class is following expectations, and I am sure to praise the entire class for their great behavior with the goal of making eye contact and smiling at each student.

Children respond to praise.

It is also significant to teach children to praise themselves. At times say, "You must be so proud of yourself for studying so hard and getting an A on your test." It is great for children to know that their parents are proud of them and just as great for children to feel proud of themselves. Great relationships are the foundation for success in a child's life. Knowing that you are proud encourages a positive parent/child relationship, and a positive self-esteem emerges (or positive relationship with self) when children can learn to be proud of themselves. Praise is a powerful tool in guiding human behavior at any age!

Special Time. Dedicate fifteen minutes a day (or more) and focus completely on your child, doing something that your child enjoys (ex. sitting on the floor and playing with your child and his/her favorite toys or lying across your teen's bed and interrupting homework time to catch up on their day). When children view you in a fond light, they are more likely to want to behave in a way that is pleasing to you!

Time-out. Time-out is a technique that can be used to help teach children self-control. When your child gets frustrated, overwhelmed, or begins acting out, time-out is a place where they can go to regain control and think about a better way to handle whatever they have just experienced. It can be timed. Typically, one minute for your child's age (ex. four years old equals four minutes timeout).

Before sending your child to time-out, be sure that you state clearly, "You are going to time-out because…" Teach your children that during time-out, they should take deep breaths to calm down so that they can use their brain to think. After time-out, the child and parent should discuss the behavior and discuss a different way that the child could have handled the situation. It is great if the solutions come from the child (though they may need a little prompting). Remember, discipline is about teaching and training! You can model taking time-outs yourself when you are feeling frustrated or overwhelmed (as can be the case quite regularly as a busy parent), though your time-out duration doesn't have to mimic your age!

Redirection. Show your child what you want them to do instead of what they are doing (Ex. instead of saying, "Don't hit the baby!" say, "Touch the baby like this…" and demonstrate the way you want your child to touch the baby). We get upset at our children for making bad choices, but it is important to stop and ask yourself if you have shown your child the more acceptable way to do things.

Rewards. Reward your child for desired behavior. We want our children to be internally motivated to make good choices, but it takes time and maturity for this to occur. Different children mature in different areas at different ages. Until your child matures and is internally motivated, external rewards can be very beneficial in helping them to make good choices (ex. make good choices in the grocery store, and we will have popsicles when we get home or bring your final math grade to a B+ and I will buy the game that you have been wanting).

Grant a Privilege. When your child shows maturity, give him or her an added privilege. If you have previously had trouble with your child getting up and ready in the morning and now they are up with no problems, they may be ready to go to bed an extra fifteen minutes later. Showing increased maturity can be rewarded with age-appropriate privileges.

Lose a Privilege. When your child misbehaves, privileges can be taken away (ex. if you allow your child to stay up fifteen minutes later and they begin to drag in the mornings, then that privilege can be taken away). Watching television and playing video games are privileges. If your child misbehaved at school that day, they may not be allowed to watch television or play video games after school. (Many parents don't allow these activities during the school week at all so that their children can focus on learning, imaginative play, and physical exercise.) Children should understand that there are consequences to misbehavior and that making better choices means better consequences.

Logical Consequences. Using logical consequences involves using consequences that fit the misdeed. For example, if your child lied, then their consequence may be to go to the person that they lied to, admit the lie, and apologize. Every bad choice does not necessarily require a consequence outside of those that naturally occur. We have to work on allowing our children to experience the consequences that naturally occur from their choices (ex. if they don't do their homework, then they have to go to school with their homework undone, not have you finish it after they go to bed).

Set Expectations. Tell children ahead of time what is expected of them. Parents say, "Be good," but do children always know what this means? "Be good" is a vague statement if you have not defined what it means. If you are going to the grocery store, let children know, "We are going to the grocery store, and I expect you to stay seated in the basket and use your indoor voice. And if you ask for something and I say no, say okay and move on. Do you understand?"

Many behaviors can be curbed by setting clear expectations and attaining agreement beforehand. I always have a talk with my kids on the way to church. I ask them, "Who is going to make good choices at church today? Who is going to sit down, listen, participate, and be kind?" I get everyone's agreement to making good choices before we get to church. If they do not agree, then we have further discussion about it until everyone is on the same page. One Sunday morning, I thought it wouldn't be a big deal to skip this ritual because my kids had been consistently behaving so well. It happened to be the same Sunday morning that my youngest girl gave me the hardest time, and I had to leave out of church twice due to her whining, crying, and misbehavior! I thought my kids had outgrown the talk, but she taught me this was not the case. Kids can be very good at keeping their word when expectations are clear, and any problems that they have with the expectations are discussed ahead of time.

Set Clear Limits (Especially on Safety Issues). Get down to your child's eye level and use a calm, firm tone of voice. Tell your child what you need them to do or to not do and why. A firm tone of voice can help communicate the seriousness of your request (Ex.

Hold my hand while we cross the parking lot. There are cars all around and I don't want a car to hit you).

Use Problem-Solving Skills. Many behavioral problems can be addressed by utilizing parental detective skills. If a child is hungry, tired, or experiencing negative emotions, they are more likely to act out. Feed them, let them take a nap or have an early bedtime, process their emotions, and their behavior will likely improve. I had a mom bring her daughters to me for therapy. She told me how both of her daughters' grades had dropped and both had starting getting into trouble at school within a month of each other. I asked if something had changed at home, and initially Mom said no. As we continued to talk, Mom began to describe the pressure that she has experienced since a grandparent and great-aunt died, and her partner was incarcerated. Mom later realized that all of these events happened within the two-month period that her girls' grades and behavior had changed at school. Children don't always have the words to express the emotions that they are experiencing. When they don't have the tools or are not given the opportunity, children can begin to act out externally to deal with the negative emotions that they are experiencing internally. I gave mom the tools to allow the girls to process their experience, and their behavior and achievement improved!

There is usually a reason for children's behavior or misbehavior. If your child is cranky in the morning, they may not be getting enough sleep. An earlier bedtime could completely change your experience. If he or she is having a difficult time going to bed at night, they may need to eliminate their after-school naps or increase their after-school activity. As parents, we should look at the bigger picture and seek to understand the etiology of our children's behavior or misbehavior.

Describe how your parents handled discipline.

_____

_____

_____

_____

_____

As a child/teenager, I wanted my parents to:

_____

_____

_____

Moving forward, I will guide my children's behavior by:

_____

_____

_____

Remember to be loving and forgiving of both yourself and your children. We are all imperfect beings. Guiding your child's behavior is about helping them to develop an internal moral compass that will guide their decisions. Be compassionate, communicative, consistent, and thoughtful on your journey.

CHAPTER 4

Connection

"My natural heritage, what does it mean?
How did I come to be?
Not alone in this world but connected to more;
the story of my existence...what is it for?"
Dr. Teandra Gordon

Humans are relational beings. We thrive when we are in connection and have the experience of existing bonded to something greater than ourselves. Connection is a key component in life. We flourish when we feel connected to our family, friends, history, and/or community.

Children are influenced by all the environments in which they interact. The participants in my work discussed feeling connected to grandparents, teachers, coaches, aunts, uncles, clergy, and other adults that spent time with them. A participant remembered:

"We were a close family. We always had aunts and uncles around, and growing up Catholic, the priest would eat at our house on Sundays."

As parents, we should be aware of the influences that are molding our children and purposefully connect our families to people and places that make a positive impact in our children's lives.

Family and Cultural History

Stories are the hallmark of our lives. Life accounts can be told from multiple perspectives. A tragedy can be viewed as triumph depending on the storyteller and the perspective that colors their voice. Understanding your story and articulating it to your children in a way that communicates triumph and hope can be the hallmark of the foundation on which they build their present and future. My family and cultural history could be told through a lens of tragedy and suffering or triumph and hope. I am extremely grateful that the storytellers in my life (my parents and grandparents) shared stories of our history through the lens of hope. As I share my family story from my own perspective, as shared from the perspective of my parents and grandparents, I hope that you will think about your own family and cultural history and how they have impacted the human being that you are today.

My Family Story

My grandparents were a significant figure in my daily life, and stories of their history define my perspective on life and people. My mother told me that when my black grandmother (though to the unskilled eye she may have appeared white), Yvonne Broussard, accompanied my mother's class on a school trip, she walked through the front door of a segregated restaurant in a remote part of Texas to take a black child to the restroom. My mother said that her teacher was frightened, but my grandmother was unafraid because the child had to go to the restroom! I descend from a history of strong and courageous women.

My Dad told me that when he was younger, his mom, Dutchie Bailey, always told him that they were taking the "shortcut" into Macy's in downtown Houston, Texas. The family was forced to enter through the basement due to segregation, but my dad had no idea until he was older. My grandmother also told my dad that the "best seats" were at the back of the bus! She shielded him from the fact that he was being treated as a second-class citizen because of the color of his skin. Though the facts were oppression, my father's truth was that he had a loving family and a bright future. I grew up infused with self-confidence with the fundamental belief that I was as good as anybody.

My great-grandparents, Frank and Loretta Broussard, were sharecroppers in Opelousas, Louisiana. They worked the land tirelessly and eventually saved enough money to purchase all eighty acres of land from their white landowners. My grandfather told me that it was hard work growing up on their property, but it was their own, and they worked the land with a sense of pride and accomplishment. Following my grandfather's time in the military, he and my grandmother settled in Houston, Texas, where my grandfather got a job working for a steel company. My grandmother cared for their six children at home. My grandfather became active in politics and was a passionate advocate for equality. Any politician that wanted to be elected in Houston, Texas, knew that they needed the support of the Pleasantville Civic League, and many sought to build a close relationship with my grandfather, Onesopher Broussard. My family has strong ties to the community, and our family name is defined by hard work and honor.

My grandparents worked to instill a sense of confidence and integrity in their young family. Post Brown vs. Board of Education, Houston Independent School District refused to allow my aunt to attend a school that was closer to home and better equipped because the grade that she was entering was not yet integrated in HISD. The district had also started a building project that would further segregate the students. My grandparents brought a civil rights lawsuit against HISD. I have a newspaper clipping of my mom and her siblings marching down the streets of Houston, Texas, to stand up for their rights. Advocacy, equality, and action are part of my DNA!

My dad and his cousin told me how my grandfather, Primas Napoleon Bailey, made them watch PBS documentaries daily while the rest of their friends were playing. My grandfather also required them to read aloud an article from the newspaper each morning before they were allowed to play. Education is a hallmark of my existence. I look for opportunities to learn each day.

The story of my family also includes my maternal grandmother's experience with alcoholism. There was a period in her life when she and her family dealt with the devastation, instability, and erraticism of addiction. If my family story was colored in defeat, then I could stop there and harp on the pain that was endured through this experience, but like Maya Angelou articulated, "Still I rise!" My family's story is one of hope, and I choose to be defined by its optimism. My grandmother became sober, and her sobriety helped me to grow up aware of my biological disposition to addiction. I learned from her experience, and the torment of addiction has haunted my family no more. Our family stories will not be filled with lilies and lollipops but can always end in triumph. The legacy of my grandparents and great-grandparents permeates my being each day. I wrote this poem in my early twenties when I began to embrace, understand, and articulate who I am.

Who Am I?

I am a woman after God's own heart; I love
Him, I live Him, I breathe Him
I view all human beings through His loving eyes;
I love them with his non-judgmental love;
I am also an African-American woman; I am from
a heritage of fighters and overcomers.
My ancestors were forcefully removed from their homeland
and brought to America with chains and whips
They were oppressed, but they later broke free
I learn because of their struggle, I rise because of their strength
I know who I am and I know where I come from

I, as a mother, descend from mothers who
were separated from their children;
They gave birth to the reality that their chil-
dren's freedom was not their own
I descend from fathers who were beaten and emasculated
simply because of the color of their skin
Their sons answered the white folk with,
"Yes, sir," and "Yes, ma'am."
They bowed their hands not to offend,
They lived with an uncertainty of safety, but they took a stand
Leaders rose up;
They marched, they sang, and they preached
until their voices were heard
Separate was inherently unequal
They were beaten, hosed, and imprisoned
But through patience, love, and Christ, change came forth
And here I stand—a product of their victory
I sit in the best integrated classrooms and rise to the top of my class
My mothers and fathers were forced to sit at the back,
but they sacrificed so that I could have a choice, and where do I sit?
...at the front.
I am a child of the most High God and a descen-
dant of African-American kings and queens
I take full advantage of Dr. King's dream come true
and my grandparents' decision to fight and not surrender
To those who came before me...thank you!
Thank you for your sacrifice, thank you for your vision,
thank you for your commitment, and thank you for the dream.

What is your family story? Take a minute to articulate it. Articulate it through the lens of triumph. Though there were trials, hurt, and maybe some bad decisions...here you are. You have the opportunity to use your story to fill your children with connectedness and purpose.

Take a minute to journal about your family story.

_____

_____

_____

_____

_____

Now begin to share pieces of your family story with your children as they are developmentally ready to understand.

The Significance of Family

Grandparents and extended family members add depth, history, and perspective to children's lives. Participants in my research repeatedly discussed the impact that relatives had on their development.

"We had a lot of family around all the time. Just not my mom and dad, but their brothers and sisters were always around, so that had a lot of influence on me growing up."

"I think both of my parents valued the importance of family and putting family first and appreciating the value of family."

"Grandfather, I think that was the person that I idolized the most—in part because I was around him most growing up."

"Major influences were, in the younger ages, I guess I would have to say my parents and also my grandparents...I saw my grandparents a lot. Both my mom's parents and my dad's parents lived in the same neighborhood, so I guess the whole family atmosphere...Growing up in a black

family and going to a school that is mostly white…you go to your family, and they hear that you are learning about certain things, and they might try to give you different perspectives, especially on history. Grandpa would be, like, 'So y'all are learning about so and so…well, you know, it really happened like this…'"

"Being really close to my extended family, like my cousins and my aunts and my uncles, was always really important to me. For me now, as a parent, [it is really important] to make sure that my daughter continues to interact with her family and have close relationships with them."

Extended family members added richness and perspective to the lives of the parents that I interviewed. Parents continually discussed the significance of family relationships, creating positive family memories and transmitting a love and commitment to family to the next generation. The participants remembered holidays, "get-togethers," and learning that with family, it's imperative to "always love each other."

"My mom would always get excited about the holidays because that was family time, and we would see our extended family. She would make such a big deal about that and get everybody in the holiday spirit. I have these memories, which I think are truly invaluable. Now I do that and kind of drive everybody crazy about the holidays and the preparation, and I want to do this, this, and this…We always enjoyed food and coming around the table, and whenever we would go to someone else's house, it was always centered around food and talking and bringing back memories. Especially growing up with both my great-grandma and my great-grandpa, we got to learn a lot about the past history and the lives of black people growing up. It was just amazing to be able to talk to people from that generation and to get that experience."

These childhood experiences translated into the connection that the parents wanted their own children to have with their family.

"They love their family, and they love being with their family…and that warms my heart."

A parenting couple expressed:

"It came out in different ways, but we were both very loved and cared for. We both had good childhoods and understand the importance of family."

"I was a kid that said that I wanted to have four children (two girls and two boys) because I wanted my children's children to have biological aunts and uncles because I do. My mom has five brothers and sisters, so I get [biological aunts and uncles]. So that's been important to me because I don't want the closeness of family that we had to die somewhere. [My kids] love their family, and they love being with their family, and that warms my heart."

Your life may or may not be full of the warm childhood memories with family members that many of the participants in my work described. Some people grew up in very toxic environments that were embedded with abuse and secrets. One valuable lesson that I learned early in life is that some people need to be loved from a distance. Forgiveness is important because it frees you to live your life without carrying the negativity of your experience each day. Forgiveness does not mean that you will be in close relationship with those that you have forgiven. With some family members, you may need to wish them well…from a distance.

In other cases, parents may be emotionally cutoff from their families, and the relationships are repairable. Don't run from someone just because loving them takes a little extra work.

Children become more resilient and emotionally intelligent when they learn to navigate relationships with diverse personality types. There may be family members that you should consider reconnecting with. Retaining strong family bonds in this busy stage of life takes effort. I challenge you to check your heart and check your family connections. Determine for yourself and your children if reconnecting with family members is best or if you should just love your family from a distance. Remember that the best choices in life are often the ones that take the greatest effort.

What extended family members are you closest to?

_____

_____

_____

Which family members do you need to forgive? Why?

_____

_____

_____

Which family members should you consider reconnecting with?

_____

_____

_____

What is your plan to reconnect?

_____

_____

_____

CHAPTER 5

Values

"As I make choices, whose hand do I hold?
Who guides this life of mine, and what is it for?
The truths that I hold, determined by you; teach
me and show me…what should I do?"
—Dr. Teandra Gordon

It is difficult to navigate life without a moral compass to light our path and guide our decisions. "Who am I?" and "Why am I here?" are questions that we ask ourselves. Life can be challenging, unpredictable, and comprised of both tragedy and triumph. We are imperfect beings in need of strength, wholeness, and hope. A participant in my work shared:

"I know some people don't believe in a higher power, but you have to have something in your life that you believe in."

Have you heard the saying, "If you don't believe in something, you'll fall for anything"? Life can be navigated when we experience belief beyond ourselves.

I have heard parents take the road that says, "I don't want to push faith on my children. I want them to decide what they believe for themselves." This mindset is admirable, but it devalues the insight of parents, grandparents, and the wisdom that has been passed on through life experiences. If you are a parent who is unable to answer the questions, "Who am I?" and "Why am I here?" I challenge you to find out so that you can teach your children. It is unfair to have children enter the world without purpose, meaning, and a power to believe in that is greater than themselves. Life can be challenging, and human hearts are fragile. It is important for us to have greater belief to anchor our souls during difficult times.

I have had therapy clients that were born attractive with great gifts and abilities and wonderful intellects, but they lacked the spiritual fortitude to endure life's setbacks. Spirituality is a significant aspect of the human existence and should be nurtured and developed. Intellect, ability, and attractiveness can take us to great places, but it takes spirituality, character, and values to sustain us.

Kids become what they behold. It is significant for parents to live according to the values that they want transmitted to their children. Role modeling is the greatest teacher.

"I always had a sense of right and wrong, and it was, of course, based on our faith, our religion, and growing up and going to church. Getting a chance to hear and see your parents really emphasize that in the things that they're teaching you, the things they're telling you. You don't always receive every lesson you get as a child, but there was never a doubt as to where they were coming from or what they wanted us to put stock in."

The life that you are living before your children is the life that you are teaching them to live for themselves. Do you value honesty, hard work, integrity, excellence, compassion, teamwork, faith, service? Making choices toward action that represent your inner values is the most effective way to transmit these values to your children.

Throughout the interviews that I had with parents, the participants discussed the truths that guided their lives and learning those truths from the individuals that raised them. Whether it is a truth that they will cling to or a lesson learned from a parent's imperfections; the truths that were present in childhood colored the participant's perspective on life and parenting. We, as parents, should understand that the way that we live our lives before our children will color their perspective on life forever. We are their greatest teachers. Who we are will shape who our children will become. It is significant that as parents, we work on ourselves and live according to our values.

Children learn most from what they see. If words and actions are contradictory, such as a parent saying, "Don't use profanity," but the parent uses profanity in every other sentence, the parent's actions will speak louder than their words. Our choices not only affect our lives, but they also affect the human beings that our children will become. Parents in my work continually discussed the values that were passed on to them from their parents and how these values molded the human beings that they have become.

Hard Work and Goal-setting

"[My mother] worked two and three jobs…she busted her butt all the time. I have never been afraid of hard work because I saw her do that."

"My mom was up and out of the house before I even got up. I would leave to go to school, and [my dad] would leave to go to work right after that. So that mindset of work, of being productive, of doing something significant every day [was transmitted to me]."

If you want your children to understand the significance of setting goals and working hard to attain them, it is important to live it out before them. Let them see your inner process and understand the work that it takes to attain what you have accomplished. If there are people that you admire, learn from them yourself and then transmit that knowledge to your children through your actions. Life is a journey. As adults, we are continually learning. The greatest gift that we can give to our children is to live our best life and to transmit our positive tools and truths to our children.

A participant whose parents immigrated to the US so that he and his siblings could have a better life expressed:

"I watched [my parents] lead by example because they were the ones taking on the unknown. [They always told me] no matter what it is, you have to work for it. You have to work towards your goal and go out and achieve it and then set another one."

We were each created with destiny and purpose, but it takes sacrifice to reach our goals. If we want our children to set goals and work hard to accomplish them, this value is best transmitted through our example.

Sacrifice

A participant shared:

"My mother always gave us the best, and she went without, so I learned self-sacrifice. For me, I'm willing to sacrifice anything for my kid."

Becoming a parent means that life is not about me; it's about us. There is a lifestyle change that happens when we make the transition into parenthood. I learned the selfless love of a mother from the way that my parents loved me. I have a brief story about my mom and my dad that represents the sacrificial love that they transmitted to me.

My Mom: My mom always worked but never seemed to have enough money for everything in the month. She wanted me to attend a fancy holiday formal during my second year in college. I had planned not to attend because I didn't have money for a dress. My mom sent me the money! I later learned that her lights were cut off because she gave me money for that dress. That sacrificial love is something that my mother transmitted to me. I learned the internal satisfaction that I receive from putting my children's needs before my own.

My Dad: My parents divorced when I was five years old. It was the most difficult experience of my life. If anyone asked me to make three wishes, the first would always be, "I wish my parents would get back together." My dad sacrificed by choosing not to remarry when we were kids because he couldn't fathom the idea of caring for another woman and her children while my brother and I felt like guests in his home.

These two stories are not necessary for others to replicate to express sacrificial love for their children. These are my stories. Our caregivers are not perfect beings, but I hope that you were loved sacrificially by someone in your life.

Take a moment to jot down your own story of sacrificial love.

_____

_____

_____

In what ways have you expressed sacrificial love to your children?

_____

_____

_____

Church and Values

In my research, parents continued to value their faith in context of the life lessons that were gained from childhood experiences.

"I would say the biggest thing is really me being active in church. That's where a lot of my values came from. My mom made sure I was at church every Sunday, during the weekly Bible classes. She tried to

expose me to different things, but my church played a big part in my life growing up."

"Church was like a safe haven for us. Both of my parents were in the military, so they didn't have any family where I grew up, and the church members became our family."

"My church played a big part in my life growing up. Even when my mom stopped bringing me, my pastor's wife stepped in and would come and get me and bring me to Sunday school. [There were] individuals at church that I kind of looked up to. They went to college, and they would come back and tell their stories."

"The involvement in the congregation played a huge role in my development—learning Bible stories, scripture quoting, speaking at different events—that played a huge role in preparing me to do different things in the world."

Our children are influenced by all the environments in which they interact. If you are fortunate enough to find a congregation that represents the values that you hold and the values that you want passed on to your children, this can be an additional avenue of shaping their worldview and values. It is significant to be purposeful in selecting the environments that influence your child's development.

Faith and Balance

A participant described her experience with Christianity and how she wanted to transmit these beliefs to her children.

"I think balance is important. I think whatever you do in life, it should be balanced and not to the extreme. You can get overzealous in some things, and it pushes people away. The Bible and the church were used as forms of punishment (whenever we were in trouble we had to read a

book in the Bible). So I think for a while that pushed me away from the church because I associated it with all of this negative stuff. Now I appreciate being grounded in Christianity, and I want my kids to be grounded in it too, but I don't want to use that as a tool where they see it as a tool for anything. I want them to believe because they want to believe and they see the good in believing.

"When we were first growing up, it was like there is no choice. You receive Jesus or you're going to hell. I think [my parents] had stages. As we got older, we learned how fear turned to reverence. [We learned] why you should love and serve God. [My parents] came from a background where it was church, all church, God, nothing else. "They grew up in an environment where going to the movies was wrong, and this was wrong, and that was wrong. I think they did the best job they could of allowing us to still develop as kids and adolescents and to do things that kids do. Even though my dad didn't play sports (he worked his whole life), he allowed us to do that.

"I want my daughter to have a very strong spiritual foundation, but I wrestle with religion as opposed to my husband who functions better with organized religion. I'm the rebel. I'll go out by the lake and pray, and that can be my church, I don't need to be in church. So I know that I want her to have a strong sense that there's something bigger than her, that she has a purpose, and that everything is exactly as it's supposed to be, but I haven't quite figured out how I want to help her learn those things. I think from her dad, she'll get it through the church and the structure and reading her Bible and that sort of thing. And from me, I guess I want her to know that is great and wonderful but that God isn't just in church— he's everywhere. That being respectful of other people and valuing nature and animals, it's all part of connecting with that higher power. That is extremely important. I think that is the most important thing."

Balance is significant. Through communication and compassion, you can find the balance that is right for your family and your faith. As parents, we must also balance high standards and compassion, expectations and forgiveness, pursuit for greatness and acknowledgement of imperfections. Finding this balance will help sustain an optimistic spirit for both ourselves and our children.

Faith and Decision-Making

Another participant discussed her goal of having her kids "grounded" in Christianity. She said:

"[I want] their Christianity [to be] a big part of [their] life, their everyday decisions, how they treat other people when it comes to making right or wrong decisions. I would like for what we try to teach them to help navigate them in that area."

Another participant agreed that he wanted his children "encompassed [in] God's love" and that he wanted his kids to understand that "God is here to take you on a journey that nobody else can take you on." These parents described their faith in a tangible way. They expressed wanting their children to be "grounded" in their faith and to utilize these values as a moral campus on how they make decisions.

Any faith should be taught under the reality that we are imperfect. Mistakes and bad choices are a reality in life, and it is important for us to embrace imperfection. I have seen many teenagers distraught over the regret of bad choices. They become stuck in the darkness of depression because they made a poor decision or experienced rejection.

I experienced depression in my own life. At age sixteen, I had high standards for myself and made a choice that fell below these standards. I was devastated. During this difficult time in my life, my parents were present, involved, and compassionate. One night, my dad held me and prayed for me all night as I cried. Through this experience, I developed a personal relationship with God that continues to this day. Perfection is not required, and our paths won't be straight and free from disappointment. Living authentically is key to an authentic faith that can enhance the human experience and not serve as a weight, hindrance, or barrier to genuineness and love. As parents, we must set the standard for excellence but allow for disappointment and mistakes as our children grow and develop.

Authenticity and Values

You are only teaching your children values that you are living honestly before them. Children learn best through role modeling. They do what they see, and they become what they behold. It is important for parents to find truth in their own spiritual journey and to live that truth authentically before their children. The more that we are grounded in the reality of our own identity, purpose, destiny, and truth, the more that we can transmit these values to our children.

Take a moment to brainstorm the core values that you want to pass on to your children. Now think about how you can exemplify these values each day as you parent *with purpose*.

Value 1:

_____

_____

_____

How I can demonstrate this value in my life:

_____

_____

_____

Value 2:

_____

_____

_____

How I can demonstrate this value in my life:

_____

_____

_____

Value 3:

_____

_____

_____

How I can demonstrate this value in my life:

_____

_____

_____

Value 4:

_____

_____

_____

How I can demonstrate this value in my life:

_____

_____

_____

Value 5:

_____

_____

_____

How I can demonstrate this value in my life:

_____

_____

_____

Value 6:

_____

_____

_____

How I can demonstrate this value in my life:

_____

_____

_____

Value 7:

_____

_____

_____

How I can demonstrate this value in my life:

_____

_____

_____

Value 8:

_____

_____

_____

How I can demonstrate this value in my life:

_____

_____

_____

Value 9:

_____

_____

_____

How I can demonstrate this value in my life:

_____

_____

_____

Value 10:

_____

_____

_____

How I can demonstrate this value in my life:

_____

_____

_____

CHAPTER 6

Education

*"How will I view the world? Through what lens
will I see? As I learn and gain wisdom,
what type of human will I be?"*
—Dr. Teandra Gordon

Education is the acquisition or transmission of knowledge and wisdom. To educate is to foster the development of reasoning and judgment and to prepare for life. Education exists in many forms— through both experiences and impartation. The participants in my work discussed education in terms of exposure to academics, extra-curricular activities, travel, and culture. Our lives are the illustration of our inner knowledge acquisition. A child's education is a key component of development.

Education as a virtue was transmitted through my family. My ancestors were limited in their outward acquisition of wealth, but their inner acquisition of knowledge could not be stripped. My aunts and uncles were college-educated, which made college an expectation for me.

Children's thoughts, perceptions, and expectations are shaped by influential individuals in their lives. Children are also molded by the environments in which they interact. Exposing your children to environments and individuals that broaden their scope of expectation and nurture their inner curiosity defines their hope for existence.

Academics

Whether your parents were like some participants in that,

"B's are not acceptable, because you didn't work hard enough."

"It was one of those kinds of homes where you don't bring home below a B. [My dad always said] if you want to do well in life you have to get a good job, if you want to get a good job, you have to get a good education."

Or like others in that,

"I wish somebody would have stressed education. I wish I would have had a strong person that really knew the value of education because I think I had the [intelligence] to be further along in life. I'm trying to do it now because I understand, but had I had that person there to nurture, then I could have been a lot further than I am today."

Parental perspectives and action regarding education have a significant impact on each child's educational attainment. The first words that come to mind when many hear the word *education* is academics or school. There are many options for school in today's society. There are public schools, charter schools, online schools, private schools, parochial schools, home schools, Montessori schools, classical schools, and the list goes on and on. As parents, it is important that we take agency in our children's education and understand that their learning is ultimately our responsibility. After the examination of our own values regarding education, we must make choices that align with our family's educational goals and with what fits with our children's individuality as learners. A vital component of any educational environment is caring, informed, and passionate educators. A participant in one of my studies expressed,

"You can't hide things from [good] teachers. They can tell when a kid has potential, especially when [teachers] are really into their jobs. I think [my teachers were] part of the reason that I was able to break my mold and come out and be the student that I knew I could be. If I didn't put forth my best, then they were quick to come down on me and say 'Hey, you need to do more.'"

Outside of caring, informed, and passionate teachers and school leaders, there are not many "good" or "bad" choices regarding educational options. There are choices that are best for our children and the environment that they need for optimal development.

My Own Story

My dream for my children's education stemmed from my personal experiences. I grew up in a public school system in the Houston, Texas area and had a wonderful educational experience. I excelled academically in many ways and won numerous awards yearly, including top scholar athlete and being voted "Most Intelligent Girl" in my senior year in high school. Despite these accomplishments, I did not push myself academically. I had a great all-around experience, enjoying my time as an athlete and in my youth group at church, but I didn't give my best academic effort. Throughout school, academic success came easy for me due to intellect without the addition of hard work. I realized in my first year in college (after making more than one C!) that I actually needed to study and didn't know how. My freshman year in college also came with spiritual challenges. I grew up in church but wasn't grounded in the truths associated with my faith. I made negative choices that left me feeling broken as a woman. I knew that my life would be spent giving to others, so a couple of weeks before I was set to begin my sophomore year at Baylor University, I decided instead to attend a non-accredited Bible College in Broken Arrow, Oklahoma. Through my time at Rhema Bible Training Center, I grew spiritually and became rooted, grounded, and knowledgeable spiritually. I became a leader and emerged ready to make a positive contribution to humanity.

My developmental experiences formulated the dream that I have for my children's education. I want them to be both nurtured and challenged in an academic environment in which they can simultaneously grow intellectually, spiritually, and physically. I want them to be challenged academically and learn that success emerges through focus and effort. I want my children's development to be an integrated process. I have pursued private education for my children in Christian environments. Because of my dream, I have humbly applied for financial aid to send my children to schools that I could not afford. I share my story not to inspire parents to pursue similar educational pursuits for their children but to encourage parents to examine their own educational experiences and determine their educational goals, values, and dream for their children. I want parents to think and dream outside the box and take agency in their children's education.

Agency Is Important

I admire the agency that I have seen in parents as they determine the best educational environment for their children. I have seen families with children that are struggling to sit still and abide with the expectations in public school, find private schools, charter schools, and home school programs that meet their children's needs. Discovering the right educational environment for your child's personality, temperament, and skills is worth the sacrifice if it fits your child's educational needs.

"So we are a divided home. I'd like a private school, he wants a public school. His education was great, my education was great. Private schools have smaller classroom sizes, and I think there is something to be said for all of your teachers knowing your name, knowing who you are, knowing when you're present and when you're not present. In public school, it's

everything. It's good, it's bad, it's everything. It is who your kid is, how they're raised, and partial luck that keeps them from navigating into the wrong thing. And then also the whole testing thing, I don't want her to learn a test. There's so much more to learn than what is on those standardized tests. Even if you can pass the tests and you don't know what the continents are and where Asia is, then to me, you're not a well-rounded individual. And you go to college with such limited knowledge. That's scary to me. I guess I feel really strongly about this."

There are benefits in all types of learning environments. I grew up in an extremely diverse public school, both economically and culturally. I credit my experience at North Shore High School for nurturing my ability to connect with all kinds of people. I see the common thread in humanity and can sit across the table, communicate, and relate with people from diverse backgrounds. There are few "right" or "wrong, "good" or "bad" educational options. There are options that are "right" for your family.

Whether you choose private school, public school, charter school, or home school, parental involvement is a key predictor of children's success. Long gone are the days when you just drop children off at the local school and say, "Teach them." Learning happens every day, and our children learn best in an environment where parents are supportive and connected. Research shows that if we want our children to go to college, we must impart this value at an early age and convey the value of education to our children in everyday experiences.

A research participant identified his family's relationships with education.

"I wanted to joke and play and run with my friends and do some of the things that they were doing, but it was an expectation and a standard [regarding education] that was set so long ago that I never really knew any different. I guess if you instill something in a child early enough, they don't even feel pressure or some of the weight that bears on them because

that's just the life they have. I think about children in other cultures. If you look at the academic standards that are put on children in other countries, you're expected to know at least three languages if you grow up in certain parts of Africa. You're expected to know at least two languages if you grow up in Mexico or anywhere else because they know that the language of business is English. I don't even think it's an obstacle. It's a standard that's been set down, so I'm big on that as well. As a parent, I realize the importance of setting a standard and making sure that we never even make [education] feel like an option."

If your child's education is important to you, convey this value in everyday interactions.

Reading to young children and speaking to them in grammatically correct sentences is a start. Parents are the first teachers. Teach your children at every opportunity. Children don't know unless they are taught through words or actions. For me, grades are not as important as effort. I expect my children to prepare, give their all, and do their best at every endeavor that they undertake. If their best gets a grade of B, then I am extremely proud of them.

In my work, the participants with parents who stressed education excelled academically.

There were male research participants who said that their parents stressed manual labor and learning a trade. They reported wishing that their parents had stressed education because had it been important to their parents, it would have been important to them. A participant remarked:

"Education wasn't really a big thing."

Another participant shared:

"My dad had this thing to where, I guess as a man, you're going to make a way. So he didn't push education on my brother and me, but the girls, they always had to come home with the A's and the B's. I think his thought

process was that for us, we could go get a job at a shipyard. We could do manual labor with no problems."

For children to excel academically, they should experience educational opportunities that meet their needs and mirror parental values. Parents should stay involved in their children's education. Parents should help children set academic goals and set the expectation for children to study, work hard, and do their best. Children's values regarding education are first shaped by the values that are expressed by their parents.

What were the positive things about your educational experience growing up?

_____

_____

_____

What do you wish had been different about your educational experience?

_____

_____

_____

What is your dream for your children's education?

_____

_____

_____

Tips to Finding the Right School:

- Research schools in your area online, through other parents, community members, clergy, etc. Share the dream that you have for your child's education and learn about other's experiences with various options (do not base your decision on one family's experience, but gather lots of perspectives before ruling out particular educational options).
- Reach out to school leaders and request appointments to discuss what their school has to offer your child (and the dream that you have for your child's education).
- Do not rule out schools because they require tuition. Investigate about financial aid, if needed.
- Don't rule out schools simply because of their reputation. Give each option a fair chance.

Meet with leaders to inquire about their vision and determine if it lines up with your own.

Tips for Promoting Academic Success for Your Child: Preschool

- Read to your kids daily. Use expression (voices for characters). Make reading enjoyable.
- Choose educational television shows. Don't allow your kids to watch mindless or developmentally inappropriate television.
- Choose learning games on electronic devices.
- Teach your children letters and sounds.
- Believe in them. Call them smart (infuse them with self-esteem).
- Consider signing your child up for a preschool program (by three or four years old, children should be learning consistently).

Elementary

- Help your child solve problems and develop positive study habits (ex. study for spelling tests each day instead of cramming the night before).
- Be clear and consistent with expectations and consequences. Set limits regarding routines, including TV, video games, and bedtime.
- Meet teachers, staff, and understand learning goals. Request meetings with teachers and ask what role you can play in promoting your child's learning.
- Continue reading enjoyable books to your child. As your child learns to read, take turns reading to each other.
- Support your child in taking on new challenges. Encourage him or her to find solutions to problems.
- Promote self-esteem and self-efficacy. Use positive words to describe your child and their experience. ("You are smart. I know you can do it. Don't give up.")
- Talk to your child about college. Take them to college events (search the Web site of your local colleges and find developmentally appropriate activities).

Middle School

- Spend time with your child. Instill a sense of hope and optimism about their future.
- Stay involved with your child's school. Go to events and develop trusting relationships with teachers and school staff. Share with school staff your dream for your child and ask how you can support your child's learning in the classroom.
- Work to build relationships with your child's friends and their families. Encourage your child to choose friends with similar interests and goals.

- Encourage your child to set goals and act each day to reach them.
- Encourage daily reading and studying.
- Talk to your child about college and choices that they should make now if college is their goal.
- Show your child unconditional love and spend fun time together as a family.

High School

- Talk to your teen about college. Take them on college visits.
- Meet and get to know your teen's friends and their families (as much as possible).
- Stay interested and involved in your teen's school life and extracurricular activities.
- Encourage your teen, compliment them, and let them know that you believe in them.
- Create opportunities to communicate with your teen in a relaxed environment. Listen to your teen and value their opinions and ideas. It is significant that they feel heard.

Extracurricular Activities

Education was expressed by participants in my work in terms of exposure to extracurricular activities.

"We're trying to determine what their loves are so that we can focus them in the right way, so that when they grow up, they can do something that they love and that they're passionate about."

Extracurricular activities provide children with the opportunity to have diverse experiences and stay busy with positive pursuits. Have you heard the old saying, "An idle mind is the devil's playground"? The right extracurricular activities can help to fill children's time outside of school with positive endeavors. The right activities add excitement to kids' lives so that kids are not looking for excitement in drugs, sex, alcohol, the Internet, negative peer influences, and other negative pastimes.

"When I look back at it, piano really saved my life. I grew up in the ghetto. I would have to break away [from hanging with my friends on the streets] and go to choir rehearsal. They would call me 'church boy.' I grew up with them, so they loved me and knew me, but I was never really a part."

"My involvement in extracurricular activities, [particularly] sports and a spelling competition—those type of things—helped remove me from one element to help me get in a better element and proceed forward."

These participants viewed extracurricular activities as an avenue to a diverse peer group and a greater expansion of possibilities. Extracurricular activities can also contribute to self-esteem and helping children realize their gifts. How would Michael Phelps have become the most decorated Olympian of all time had he never entered the pool? How would Simone Biles, Gabby Douglas, Laurie Hernandez, Madison Kocian, and Aly Raisman have realized their gifts in gymnastics had they never been exposed? A participant shared:

"The more we expose them to, the more we know what their likes and dislikes are. We're trying to determine what their loves are so that we can focus them in the right way, so that when they grow up, they can do something that they love and they're passionate about. Anyone who does something that they love, they're better at it; they become more successful at it."

Your child will never become a world-class cello player if they were never introduced to the cello in the first place. Extracurricular activities can be a fun way for kids to explore new possibilities or just an exciting way to spend their time!

Tips for promoting extracurricular activities:

- Brainstorm possibilities with your child (martial arts, instruments, sports, robotics, etc.).
- Research opportunities on the Internet, speak to other parents, school personnel, clergy, and observe what is present in your area.
- Places like the YMCA can provide multiple extracurricular opportunities and financial assistance to families that need it.
- Encourage your child to participate in extracurricular activities when they are offered at school (especially in middle school and high school). This promotes connection to the school environment, which is associated with greater emotional health, school satisfaction, school completion, and academic success.

Exposure

Parents also discussed education in terms of exposing children to diverse people, places, and ways of life to expand their frame of reference. A participant shared:

"I think exposure, giving your kids the opportunity to see different things, [is important]. A lot of kids are in a home where they never get to experience anything outside of their surrounding neighborhood. So we try to take [our kids] different places and show them different parts of the world where they can ask questions and understand how people do things versus just how we do it. And [we want] to give [our kids] the opportunity to do different things and not be just stagnant and to expose them to a bigger world than just the community that they live in.

"It is important to expose them to the right things—nice things.

"One thing I would like to do is have [my kids] with me on jobs. I think that was an invaluable experience that I was able to get from my dad. No matter how much you grow up and your parents work, there is nothing like going to work with your mom and dad."

"Exposure to parents' work environments is invaluable."

Exposure to people from other cultures was a significant factor to the parents that I interviewed. One parent remarked:

"Take [President Barack Obama] for example. This is a biracial man with an African name who was able to make it as president of the United States of America. If he wasn't able to connect with everybody, no matter what and who they look like, [he would not have been able to do that]. And just look at our most successful public figures. Whether it be politicians or athletes, the people that can cross different cultures and relate to other people, they are more successful, they are more open-minded, they are more tolerant. It's just unfortunate when you meet close-minded people, and they judge people either by the color of their skin or by their background."

Experiences with individuals that are different promotes connection. When people are able to connect with diverse groups, it increases their marketability and success. It is only by experiencing diverse cultures that an individual can truly understand the universality of the human experience and that the commonalities that bind us are stronger than the ones that divide.

The idea of exposure was summed up by a participant.

"If you don't even know what's on the other side of the bridge, how do you know that what you're doing is worth it?"

Exposing your children to diverse people, places, and experiences can be done *with purpose*. It is significant for children to identify broader possibilities for their existence. There are so many world-class gifts that have not been fostered because they were placed in children that weren't given the opportunity to discover them. Be intentional about exposing your children to diverse experiences and be open when their hearts start to flutter at a newfound passion.

Allow Your Children to Dream

One of the greatest gifts that we can give to our children is to believe in their dreams. Many parents believe that they are doing children a service when they rationalize away their child's dream. Every human being is born with a unique purpose. Our job as parents is to expose our children to diverse experiences and to allow that seed of destiny to be ignited inside of them.

Once children experience their passion, we should allow that light to lead them (with the addition of our wisdom). One of my favorite movie scenes that illustrates *amazing* parenting is the basketball scene in *The Pursuit of Happiness.* Christopher (played by Jaden Smith) tells his dad, "I'm going pro!" as they are shooting basketball. Christopher Gardner (played by Will Smith) immediately starts to rationalize away his son's dream. Little Christopher becomes visibly defeated. His father catches this and realizes that he has no right to rationalize away his son's dream. He tells young Christopher, "Don't let anyone tell you what you can't do, not even me." It is a great lesson for us all. Children are born with deposits of destiny. Our job is to nurture them, teach them, and guide them as they follow the dream from within. Their dream may shift as they grow and mature, but allowing them to dream at all stages of life keeps a fire and passion burning within them.

What dream did you have as a child?

_____

_____

_____

What did your parents do to nurture that dream?

_____

_____

_____

What do you wish your parents had done to nurture your dream?

_____

_____

_____

What is your child's dream?

_____

_____

_____

What will you do to nurture your child's dream?

_____

_____

_____

CHAPTER 7

Special Topics

"I can't believe this happened. Can we make it through?
Challenges and triumphs building resilience and fortitude."
—Dr. Teandra Gordon

Families experience cycles, transitions, tragedy, and triumph. If what you are experiencing as a family is becoming too difficult to navigate on your own, there is no shame in getting help. It is quite admirable to admit that we are human beings, both fragile and strong.

Life can be challenging, and it is okay to need others (including professionals) to help us navigate. Continue reading for a *brief* overview of special topics that I experience regularly as I work with families in therapy.

Adoption

Many children are born to parents that do not have the intellectual, emotional, spiritual, financial, or physical ability to care for them. Adopting a child is one of the most amazing acts of selflessness and love. Each child deserves a chance to realize their unique potential. It is absolutely amazing for individuals to choose to accept a child into their home, hearts, and families. Parents can adopt children at many different stages of development, who have had diverse experiences. The biggest key is to be patient. Bonding as a family can take time, and there will be challenges along the way. When children realize that your love is unconditional and that your care for them will withstand tests and trials, they will often begin to thrive. Research as much as you can about adoption and utilize the tools in this book. You are a parent, and from this point on, just parent your child with purpose.

Blended Families

When forming a blended family, parents should be patient. Start slow and allow relationships to develop with time and experience. Love, acceptance, and a sense of family take time to develop, but respect should be an expectation. Create structure in the home and encourage respect from all involved. Children may struggle with conflicting loyalties, but don't get discouraged or take things personally. Be patient, nurturing, and consistent. Children will usually recognize and respond to kindness, consistency, and authenticity.

Parent with purpose as a biological parent:

- Maintain the primary responsibility to care for and discipline children (at least initially).
- Have special time with your child. Communicate, connect, and allow children to express their thoughts and experiences.

Parent with purpose as a stepparent:

- Don't force relationships. Establish a warm and supportive relationship with children (like a mentor, friend, or uncle/ aunt).
- Spend time together as a family and try to develop new rituals and traditions.
- Expect that there will be challenges and adjustments along the way to connecting as a family.

Death

Grief is one of the most difficult issues for me to work with in therapy. I am optimistic and believe in the ability of people to change and grow, but death cannot be changed. My work with families in the initial stage of the grieving process includes sitting with them in their sadness and being unafraid to be *with them*. Part of my motivation for becoming a therapist was experiencing my own difficulty in life and feeling as though the pain that my immediate family was experiencing was "too much" for others. I felt like people loved us from a distance because they really didn't know how to help. I became a therapist so that I could be with families during the most difficult experiences of their lives. When someone close to us dies, it is one of the true tests of our resilience.

When children experience the death of someone they love, it is important for families to realize that children may or may not have the traditional grief responses (denial, anger, bargaining, depression, and acceptance). Children will experience death in different ways depending on their developmental stage. As children enter different developmental stages, they may cycle through stages of grief because they have a new understanding of what has occurred. Children who have experienced loss need the adults in their lives to give them permission to grieve. Many times adults are so consumed with their own process that they forget to help children with theirs.

Strategies for parenting with purpose as children grieve:

- Explain death. Use clear and concise language so that children are able to understand its finality.
- Allow children to ask questions and openly express their thoughts and experiences.
- Share your personal view of the afterlife. Do you believe that your loved one is still present in some way? Can the person see or hear your child?

- Allow children to draw pictures that represent their loved one or journal about their thoughts and feelings. When my grandfather died, my son and I drew pictures of comics because when we would visit, my grandfather would sit my son on his lap and read the comics section of the newspaper to him.
- Talk to kids about what you are feeling in a developmentally appropriate way without dumping on your children. Process your experience with other adults or a therapist. Processing your own grief in a healthy way is one of the best strategies for helping children with their process.
- Allow children to write a letter to their loved one (possibly saying the things that they were not able to say or updating them on what is happening in their life).
- Get down on the floor and play with young children. Children often articulate their thoughts, feelings, and experiences when they are involved in the non-threatening activity of play.
- Stick to routines as much as possible. Kids find comfort in routines, and it helps to reinforce the idea that life will continue past the death of their loved one.
- Realize that children may have physical reactions to grief (my son vomited several times the morning of my grandfather's funeral). Children may not intellectually understand, but their grief may manifest in stomachaches, headaches, lethargy, etc. Pay attention to this and utilize the strategies above to help children process their experience.
- Understand that children are resilient. As parents, we don't want our children to experience pain, but through difficult experiences, children can learn that there is life after pain. Internalizing this truth will increase your child's compassion and resilience as they grow.
- Seeking professional help through therapy can be a great way to help your family process the difficulty of finding a new normal without your loved one.

Divorce

Divorce can be like death in many ways. It is the death of a child's ideals associated with their family. Both mothers and fathers contribute greatly to the well-being of children. It is comforting to know that the two people that love you most in the world live in the same house with you. My parents divorced when I was five years old, and experiences surrounding their divorce colored my childhood. In any experience where I was offered three wishes, one of them was always that my parents would get back together. I believe that couples should do everything that they can to fight for their families. There was a reason that the two people got married in the first place, and I believe that through humility, therapy, and unconditional love, couples can move back to that place. There are far too many divorces in this country, and divorce can have a profound effect on children.

Living for years and years in unhappiness with your partner is not healthy for children either. If divorce is the best option for the health of your family, then children need the opportunity to have healthy relationships with both parents without feeling as though they have to choose. Divided loyalties can be devastating for the existence of a child. Never place children in the middle of adult drama. Place your love for your children above negative feelings for your partner. Protect your children through what may be one of the most difficult experiences of both of your lives.

Parent your children with purpose through a divorce by:

- Avoid making negative comments about your ex-partner in front of your children.
- Encourage children to have a positive relationship with the other parent.
- Do not grill children for information. Ask your ex-partner.

- Do not use children as your therapist/friend. If you need to process the experience of your divorce, talk to a friend, adult family member, or therapist.
- Clearly communicate to children that the breakdown of the relationship is not their fault and that there is nothing that they can do to salvage it. Children are egocentric, and when anything is right or wrong in their world, they often attribute it as within their power to control.
- Allow children to openly discuss their thoughts and feelings about the breakdown of the adult relationship.
- Assure children that parents and children do not divorce. Stay close to your child and spend quality time with them.

Domestic Violence

When relationships involve domestic violence, loving that person from a distance may be the best option. Love should not be violent and painful. Living in homes with domestic violence can give children warped views about love. I have seen young men grow up and pursue a life of violence and "being hard" after witnessing their mothers being abused. They are helpless as children, so when they become physically stronger, these young men become consumed with not being a victim or allowing their loved ones to be victims. They prove their masculinity at every opportunity.

I have seen young women grow up and live in abusive adult relationships because their home is where they gain ideas about love. Children look for familiarity in adult relationships. and if violence is familiar, then they often pursue intimate partnerships in which violence is a norm. If your home is a home in which you or your children live in fear of safety, it is not a healthy home to grow in. Safety is a basic need. Take a look at Maslow's hierarchy of needs below.

Without safety, children are unable to grow optimally and attain higher needs.

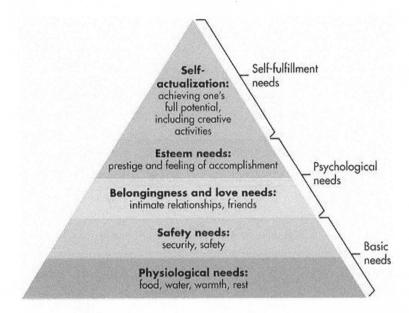

Children who have lived in homes with domestic violence need a new home experience.

They need to experience healthy love. Children need to process their thoughts and emotions through talk, play, or art, and they need to understand that what they experienced was not a healthy way of being. Children who have experienced domestic violence can become aggressive themselves because role modeling is one of the strongest teachers. They need different models for how to love and interact. In a home where children can express themselves, have healthy relationships modeled and taught, and live surrounded by love and not fear, they can heal from the effects of domestic violence and lead healthier adult lives. If you need help because you live in a home in which you fear for the safety of yourself and/or your children, call the National Domestic Violence hotline at 1-800-799-7233 or go to www.thehotline.org.

Drug and Alcohol Addiction

Addiction can be devastating to a family. Children of parents with substance abuse issues are more likely to experience physical abuse, sexual abuse, verbal abuse, and neglect. Substance abuse robs families of genuine interaction.

"[When your parents use drugs], it makes you feel neglected, left out. You feel out of place in the family. Sometimes it makes you feel mad, sad, frustrated, helpless and useless, hurt, sick. It makes you feel like you're in the middle of a war." (Quoted from an eleven-year-old child of addiction; from An Elephant in the Room by Marion H. Typpo, PhD and Jill M. Hastings, PhD)

Effects of addiction in a child's life can be viewed in terms of Maslow's Hierarchy of Needs above. When basic needs of safety are not met, then it is difficult for children to reach their potential.

Children of substance abuse often have:

- Difficulty trusting their own instincts. Parental interactions are not genuine when parents are drunk or high.
- Low self-esteem. They experience their parents' substance use as more important than them. When children do not view themselves as worthy through their parents' eyes, it is difficult to develop an internal self-worth.

Children need:

- Their parents to become sober, apologize, and assure them that parental problems are not the child's fault.
- Their guardian/caregiver to understand the etiology of addiction and explain addiction in a way that the child can understand.
- Caregivers to love them, nurture them, and assure them that their parents' addiction is not their fault.
- To communicate their thoughts and feelings through talk, art, play, or journaling.

Grandparents as Parents

Grandparents as parents can happen due to death, illness, deployment, drug abuse, and/or incarceration just to name a few scenarios. The selfless act of caring for young grandchildren on a daily basis can go against the natural progression of life. Grandparents should be able to have fun with their grandkids and enjoy their company but also enjoy the solitude and freedom that can come with retirement and launching your own children. When parents are unable to care for children, grandparents are often the logical substitute because they share the love and devotion to the child. If you find yourself in this situation, be sure to:

- Take care of yourself. You can only care for your grandchildren if you first care for yourself.
- Create a support group. Caring for grandchildren takes energy and effort. Forming a solid, trusting support group can make this experience more enjoyable for all.
- Stay positive and optimistic. This is an amazing opportunity to learn from your previous parenting experiences and rear a generation with even more wisdom, understanding, and discernment.

Poverty

It can be extremely difficult when you want to provide your children with more but don't have the resources. Never give up. Utilize the programs and resources in your community and understand that who your children become is largely associated with what you deposit on the inside of them as opposed to what you buy them. Understand that your home is their safe haven, and if you make the effort to focus on what you can provide and follow the wisdom in this book, there is no limit to what your children can become.

Sexual Abuse

Current statistics estimate that one in four girls and one in six boys have experienced sexual abuse before the age of eighteen.

Parents can protect children by:

- Educate kids on their private areas and who is and is not allowed to touch them. This education should happen from the moment that children are able to talk and comprehend. Private areas are all areas that would be covered by a bathing suit.
- Teach children the anatomically correct names for their penis and vagina so that adults are clear when children tell them that they were touched inappropriately.
- Instruct your child to tell at least two trusting adults if someone touches them inappropriately. It is the hope that at least one of these adults will listen and take action to protect the child.
- Teach children to advocate for themselves and that they have control of their bodies. I don't believe in making children hug or kiss family members (such as Aunt Peggy or Uncle Joe) against their will. Children should know that their bodies are their own and that they have control over them.
- Choose caregivers wisely. Always be aware of who will be around your child at all times.
- Teach your child not to keep secrets. Keep communication open between the two of you and let children know that they can tell you anything.

If your child experiences sexual abuse, the best thing that you can do is believe them and act to protect them. Children whose parents believe them and stand with them have better long-term outcomes. Never try to forget about sexual abuse or sweep it under the rug. Notify the authorities, Child Protective Services, and seek therapy for your child, yourself, and anyone else in the family that is directly affected.

Teen Pregnancy

Teen pregnancy can be difficult for families to experience. My mom had my older sister when she was seventeen years old, and she remembers how difficult it was to see her father devastated by the news of her pregnancy. The greatest protection against teen pregnancy is close-knit families with open communication. If your teen informs you that they are thinking of becoming, or have become, sexually active, seek medical help to ensure that they are educated on how to protect themselves against sexually transmitted disease and untimely pregnancies. If your teen or their partner does become pregnant, stand with him or her and understand that life isn't over because a baby will be born. Children are a blessing. Maintain open communication and seek professional help if you and/or your teen are having challenges with communication and decisions.

Conclusion

Parenting has been the greatest and most difficult venture that I have undertaken.

Perfection in parenting does not exist. We do the best that we can with what we have. We make choices for our children in the hope that they will make great choices for themselves. I hope that the pages of this book will help you to navigate the great adventure of parenthood more informed and confident. This has been a work from the heart, and I hope that it helps your family to thrive and create happy memories together. On your journey to helping your children learn, grow, develop, dream, and reach their potential, remember that "every child is special, born with unique gifts, talents, and abilities. Children need the adults in their lives to love them unconditionally, teach them consistently, and believe in them unwaveringly. In this environment, children can *shine* as the stars they were created to be." May you have grace, patience, and unwavering hope as you foster greatness in your *stars*.

With love,
Dr. Teandra Gordon

About the Author

Dr. Teandra Gordon is a licensed marriage and family therapist, speaker, and author passionate about helping individuals and families to overcome adversity and live, love, and succeed *on purpose*! She began her career as an elementary school teacher where she became enthusiastic about equipping parents with tools for success in parenting. Dr. Gordon has years of clinical experience providing individual therapy, group therapy, family therapy, and parenting education to families through both a community health agency and private practice. She has conducted academic research that focused on identifying successful parenting strategies. Her research has been published in scholarly journals and presented at national conferences. Dr. Gordon has taught at the collegiate level and is currently the director of Therapy Services at a large community health agency in Houston, Texas. She utilizes her professional training and personal experiences to help families along the path of healing, growth, and parenting on purpose! Dr. Gordon currently resides in a suburb of Houston, Texas, with her husband, Brian, and four children—Brian II, Tiara, Tayla, and Brielle.

CPSIA information can be obtained
at www.ICGtesting.com
Printed in the USA
FSHW012039150919
62013FS